A2 Reading and Writing

Ten practice tests for the **Cambridge A2 Key for Schools**

Anna Phillips and Terry Phillips

PROSPERITY EDUCATION

© Prosperity Education Ltd. 2025

Registered offices: Sherlock Close, Cambridge
CB3 0HP, United Kingdom

First published 2025

ISBN: 978-1-915654-52-6

Original edition © Innova Content Ltd.

This publication is in copyright. Subject to statutory exception and to the provisions of relevant collective licensing agreements, no reproduction of any part may take place without the written permission of Prosperity Education.

This edition is published by arrangement with Innova Content Ltd.

The moral rights of the authors have been asserted.

'Cambridge A2 Key' and 'KET' are brands belonging to The Chancellor, Masters and Scholars of the University of Cambridge and are not associated with Prosperity Education or its products.

Designed by ORP Cambridge

For further information and resources, visit:
www.prosperityeducation.net

To infinity and beyond.

Contents

Introduction   *v*

Test 1   *1*

Test 2   *13*

Test 3   *25*

Test 4   *37*

Test 5   *49*

Test 6   *61*

Test 7   *73*

Test 8   *85*

Test 9   *97*

Test 10   *109*

Answers   *121*

A digital platform for Cambridge exam preparation

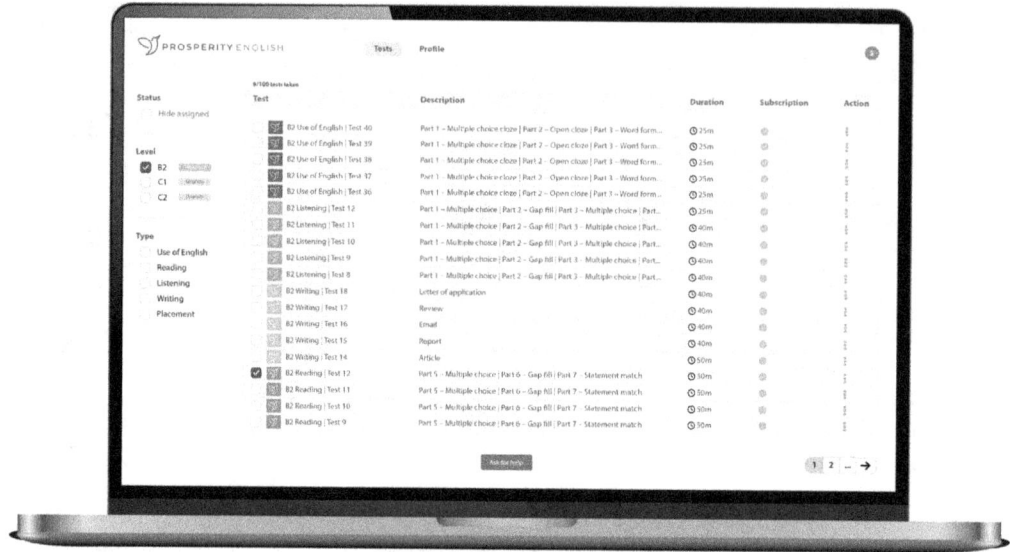

Prosperity English provides ample opportunities for repetitive practice, allowing you to reinforce your learning and improve your exam skills steadily.

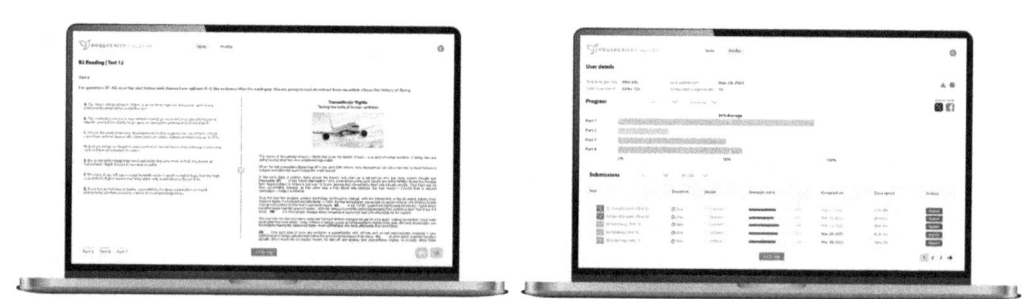

Try it for free

www.prosperityenglish.com

40% promotional discount code:
TIAB40

Introduction

Welcome to this edition of sample tests for the Cambridge A2 Key Reading and Writing, which has been written to replicate the Cambridge exam experience and has undergone rigorous expert and peer review.

The A2 Key English language exam is the second of six levels established in the Common European Framework of Reference (CEFR): A1–C2. Candidates of all ages can take the A2 Key test. In the exam you will have 60 minutes to complete the Reading and Writing paper. This section has seven parts, and is worth 50% of the final score.

The tasks include:

- answering multiple-choice questions on short and longer texts, including messages, signs, articles and websites
- completing gap-fill tasks (with and without multiple-choice options)
- writing a message using information you're given
- writing a story from three pictures.

You need to be able to:

- understand real-world messages
- read and choose the correct word
- read and choose the correct answer
- choose the correct words to complete a text
- write a message, e.g. a note or email
- write a short story.

You don't need to pass all of the papers to pass the whole exam. For example, if you do very well in the Reading and Writing paper and the Speaking paper, but you don't do so well in the Listening paper, it is still possible to pass. The Reading and Writing paper tests two skills, so this paper has double the weight of the Listening and the Speaking papers.

For more information, visit the Cambridge Assessment English website.

This book contains 10 Reading and Writing tests (Parts 1–7), comprising a total of 320 individual assessments. You or your students, if you are a teacher, will hopefully enjoy the wide range of texts and benefit from the repetitive practice, something that is key to preparing for this part of the A2 Key (KET) examination.

We hope that you will find this resource a useful study aid, and wish you all the best in preparing for the exam.

Cambridge A2 Key

Reading and Writing

Test 1

© 2025 Prosperity Education.
'Cambridge A2 Key' and 'KET' are brands belonging to The Chancellor, Masters and Scholars of the University of Cambridge and are not associated with Prosperity Education or its products.

Part 1

Questions 1 – 6

For each question, choose the correct answer.

1

> *Sorry. We are closed!*
> Hours:
> Mon–Fri: 9.00–5.30
> Sat: 9.00–4.00
> Lunch break: 1.00–2.00

You cannot buy things from this shop

A before 10.00 on Saturday.

B after 5 p.m. on a weekday.

C on Saturday at 1.30.

2

To May
From Ellen
Hi.

You know that great café we went to in town last month? Can you remember where it is? I know it's near the museum but I've forgotten the street and the number.

A Ellen wants the address of a café.

B Ellen can't remember the name of a café.

C Ellen wants to meet May in a café.

3

> **After-school clubs**
> This is to remind all students that there will be no clubs this week because there are exams in the rooms at that time.

A Students with exams can't go to an after-school club this week.

B Students can go to an after-school club this week if they don't have an exam at the same time.

C After-school clubs will not take place this week because there will be exams in those rooms.

4

What should you do?

A   Call the number to confirm thjat you want to see the bicycle.

B   Call the number to arrange a time to meet.

C   Go to the back entrance of the school to see the bicycle, then call the number.

5

Hi Jane

I've agreed to meet Sally at Meg's café at 5.00. Let me know if you can come too.

Sarah

What should Jane do?

A   Go to Meg's café at 5.00

B   Tell Sarah if she can come to the café at 5.00

C   Ask Sally if she is going to see Sarah at 5.00

6

The school play

This year we are doing a musical! Miss West is choosing the main parts at lunchtime today in the school hall.
All are welcome ... but you must be able to sing and dance.

A   Anyone can take the main parts in the school play.

B   This competition is for people who like musicals.

C   If you can sing and dance, you might get a main part in the school play.

Turn over ▶

Part 2

Questions 7 – 13

For each question, choose the correct answer.

		Emma	Holly	Sophia
7	Who comes from a big family?	A	B	C
8	Who has a long train journey to school?	A	B	C
9	Who has written a funny story?	A	B	C
10	Who wrote about a meal with her family?	A	B	C
11	Who likes to read about rockets and the planets?	A	B	C
12	Whose story teaches us something about family life?	A	B	C
13	Whose story is scary?	A	B	C

Short story competition

Send us your story with some information about you and where the idea came from.

Emma

My name is Emma and I'm 13. I have three brothers and two sisters and we have to share a lot of things, including bedrooms and clothes, so we often get angry with each other. Last week, we had a big problem with the family meal on Sunday. We each wanted something different. Finally, my mother said that we had to make the dinner ourselves and, well, the story is about what happened next. We all learnt an important lesson.

Holly

I'm Holly and I'm 12. I live with my father in a small flat near the school. I wrote about the problems my father has in understanding a 12-year-old girl. He makes strange things for dinner and always gets me strange presents for my birthday. I love sports and stories about space travel, but he bought me a doll last year and a book about horses. My story is about a birthday party which he planned for me and the funny things which happened there.

Sophia

My name is Sophia. I'm 14 and I live with my parents in a house which is a long way from the school. I have to travel on a train every day with a group of children from the school. We have had many adventures on the journey, and my story is about one of them. Something funny or interesting happens nearly every day, but I chose to write about a frightening thing which happened one day.

Turn over ▶

Part 3

Questions 14 – 18

For each question, choose the correct answer.

My grandmother's career

By Richard Black, age 12

Our English teacher asked us all to write about the working life of a person in our family. I decided to write about my grandmother, Rose, because she is the most interesting person I know.

Rose was born over 85 years ago. She grew up in a small village where there were no cars or buses and no train station for miles. There were only bicycles and lots of horses. She didn't see her first car until she was six. She was walking to the shop in the village when a sudden noise frightened her. She turned to see a car coming into the village very fast. She stopped and looked at this amazing machine. The car drove past her very fast, but suddenly it made a strange noise and stopped.

Rose walked up to get a closer look at the car. The driver had the front of the car open. He was looking at the engine, which had wires and pipes all over the place. He kept touching different parts and then, after a few moments, he said, 'Ah! That's the problem!' He pushed something hard, got back in the car and turned the key. The engine started again. As the car drove out of the village, my grandmother said to herself, 'When I grow up, I'm going to work with cars.'

She finished school and went to college, where she studied mechanical engineering. Then she got a job with a big car company and stayed with them for the whole of her working life. During that time, she was responsible for making several important improvements to car engine design.

Last week, I went to an airport for the first time and saw a plane take off. As it rose into the air, I made a decision.

14 Why did Richard choose to write about his grandmother?

    A   because she has had an interesting life

    B   because she is an interesting person

    C   because she is part of his family

15 How did she feel about the first car she saw?

    A   It frightened her.

    B   It was wonderful.

    C   It was going too fast.

16 How did the driver find the problem with the car?

    A   He opened the front of the car.

    B   He got back into the car and started it.

    C   He touched different parts of the engine.

17 What did Richard's grandmother decide as the car drove away?

    A   She wanted a career working with cars.

    B   She wanted to drive cars in the future.

    C   She wanted to own a car when she was older.

18 What did Rose do during her career?

    A   She studied mechanical engineering.

    B   She improved engine design in several ways.

    C   She became a mechanic with a top car company.

Turn over ▶

Part 4

Questions 19 – 24

For each question, choose the correct answer.

Forest Summer Camp

Do you want to be a cook when you **(19)** .... school? Perhaps you are interested in being a sports coach? Or you **(20)** .... want to teach young children to speak English. If you are interested in any of these jobs, then Forest Summer Camp is perfect for you. We offer six weeks of work this summer. We will pay you to **(21)** .... a better cook, coach or language teacher.

Children from six to ten from all over the world **(22)** .... to Forest Summer Camp each year. We teach them to speak English better, and we prepare good food for them every day. We take them to interesting places like castles and palaces, and we **(23)** .... the history of each place. We teach them to play sports – not only kicking, hitting or throwing a ball, but also playing as part of a **(24)** ....

19	A	go	B	leave	C	take
20	A	might	B	can	C	should
21	A	arrive	B	receive	C	become
22	A	bring	B	come	C	get
23	A	explain	B	say	C	talk
24	A	group	B	game	C	team

Part 5

Questions 25 – 30

For each question, write the correct answer.
Write **ONE** word for each gap.

Example: | 0 | you |

To	Michael
From	Harry

Hi Michael

I hope **(0)** .... are well. I'm having a great time here **(25)** .... Kenya. It is very hot but everything **(26)** .... exciting. Yesterday we went **(27)** .... look for big cats – lions and leopards. It was amazing! The guide took us to a lake **(28)** .... we saw a group of lions. I took hundreds of photos. I'll send **(29)** .... to you later.

Tomorrow, we're going to Mount Kenya, **(30)** .... is the second highest mountain in Africa.

More later.

Harry

Turn over ▶

Part 6

Question 31

You are going to go to the sports centre with your English friend Jo this weekend. Write an email to Jo.

Say:

- where you want to meet
- what time you want to meet
- what you want to do at the sports centre

Write **25 words** or more.

Part 7

Question 32

Look at the three pictures.
Write the story shown in the pictures.
Write **35 words** or more.

....

....

....

....

....

....

Cambridge A2 Key

Reading and Writing

Test 2

© 2025 Prosperity Education.
'Cambridge A2 Key' and 'KET' are brands belonging to The Chancellor, Masters and Scholars of the University of Cambridge and are not associated with Prosperity Education or its products.

Part 1

Questions 1 – 6

For each question, choose the correct answer.

1

Science Club
The club meeting this afternoon will not be in the Science Room because the heating will not turn on. Come to Room C31 instead at the normal time.

A   Science Club will not be in the Science Room because the room is too cold.

B   There is a problem with the heating in Room C31.

C   The Science Club is at a different time this afternoon but in the same room.

2

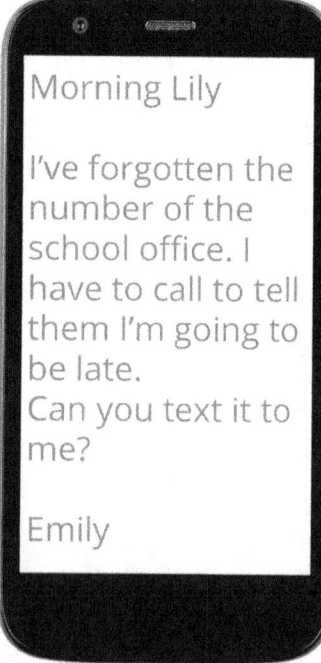

Morning Lily

I've forgotten the number of the school office. I have to call to tell them I'm going to be late.
Can you text it to me?

Emily

What should Lily do?

A   send Emily the school office telephone number

B   call the school office and tell them about Emily

C   call Emily and give her the school office telephone number

3

Black Friday!
For one day only:
Everything = 10% off
[except children's clothes]

In this shop

A   you can buy children's clothes more cheaply for one day.

B   nearly everything is 10% cheaper for one day.

C   you can get 10% off from Friday.

4

To: David
From: George

Hi
I didn't make a note of the Maths homework which we have to hand in tomorrow. Is it Exercises 1–5 on page 15 or page 18?
Get back to me soon!
George

George wants to know

A   which page the homework is on.

B   which exercise numbers to do.

C   when they must hand in the Maths homework.

5

Football computer set!

Only $20!
Everything you need to play
Football Manager AND World Cup!
Completely new!
[Birthday present but I have got it already!]
Email me at anna@outlook.com

A   The person who is selling this game set doesn't like football.

B   The game set includes two different games.

C   You must play Football Manager before you can play World Cup.

6

The school band

We need some new people for the band this year. If you can play the violin or the guitar, come to the main hall at lunchtime today. We are looking for players at an intermediate level.

A   Anyone can play in the school band.

B   The school band needs players of particular instruments who are quite good.

C   You don't have to play your instrument in the hall at lunchtime.

Turn over ▶

Part 2

Questions 7 – 13

For each question, choose the correct answer.

		Dan	Paul	Michael
7	Who uses lots of pieces of paper?	A	B	C
8	Who uses important words to remember things?	A	B	C
9	Who uses colour to remember things?	A	B	C
10	Who uses sound to remember things?	A	B	C
11	Whose bedroom is important in preparing for a test?	A	B	C
12	Who doesn't use paper in preparing for a test?	A	B	C
13	Whose way of preparing doesn't always work?	A	B	C

How do you prepare for a test?

We asked three students from the school, and this is what they said.

Dan

I always do the same thing. I write each area which will be in the test on a different piece of paper. So, for example, if it's geography of our country, I write Mountains on one piece of paper and Rivers on another one. Then I put the pieces of paper up all around my bedroom and, every time I look at a word, I try to remember all the important points. Then, in the test, I walk round my bedroom in my head to find a piece of information.

Paul

I use mind maps. I go into my bedroom and take everything off my desk. Then I get a big piece of paper and I write the most important word or phrase, like Geography, in the middle, and I draw a bubble around it. Then I write all the things which are connected to that point around it in different colours in bubbles – mountains, rivers, weather. And then I write the important facts for each thing around each bubble – again, I use different colours. When I'm doing the test, I get pictures in my head of all the main words in bubbles, and that helps me to remember the important facts. It really works!

Michael

I find that music helps me remember things. I play music all the time when I'm preparing for a test. I choose my favourite songs, then I just play the songs and read and read and read. In the test room, I play them in my head. I can often join a song with important facts. For example, I think, when I was playing that song, I was reading about mountains. Now, what is the highest mountain in my country? And, sometimes, the song helps me remember the facts. Sometimes! It's not a perfect way of preparing.

Turn over ▶

Part 3

Questions 14 – 18

For each question, choose the correct answer.

A young life on the stage

Clare White is only 14, but she has already been in 10 plays in London theatres.

Clare started acting at the age of 4 in plays at her nursery school. 'The plays were only for parents, and I couldn't act well then,' she told me, 'but for some reason, the teacher always chose me for the main part.' It seems that she was tall for her age, so perhaps that was why she was chosen.

During her first year at primary school, she was in the school play. As always, she was given the main part. Most of the people who came to watch were parents, and one of those parents was called Mike Brown. He put on plays in London and he was looking for a young child to star in his next show. He thought that Clare was a perfect actor and dancer but, for his show, he needed someone who could sing, so Mike paid for lessons.

'I wasn't very good in that first play in London,' she said, 'but I remembered all my words, and I sang my songs quite well.' The people in the theatre loved her, and someone wrote a very nice piece about her in the newspaper the next day. It was the start of her acting career.

'It's hard at times,' she says. 'I still have to go to school, so I can only act for a few hours each week during school time. It is a little easier in the school holidays, but it will be very hard next year because I have important exams.'

Perhaps Clare's life is going to become more difficult. Mike has just asked her if she is interested in doing a Hollywood film this summer.

14 Why did Clare get the main parts at nursery school?

  A   because the plays were only for parents

  B   maybe because she was a tall girl at 4

  C   because she was good at acting

15 Why did Mike Brown come to see the play in Clare's first year at primary school?

  A   He put on plays in London.

  B   He was looking for a young child to star in his play.

  C   His child was at the same school.

16 What did Mike Brown pay for?

  A   acting lessons

  B   singing lessons

  C   dancing lessons

17 How does Clare feel about her first play in London?

  A   She didn't sing very well.

  B   She didn't act very well.

  C   She forgot her words.

18 Why will next year be harder than this year for Clare?

  A   because she has to do lessons at the same time as acting

  B   because she has to act during the school holidays

  C   because she has to study for exams

Turn over ▶

Part 4

Questions 19 – 24

For each question, choose the correct answer.

Sports Day

We had a very good Sports Day last week. The weather was beautiful, and more than 200 parents came to **(19)** .... the boys and girls from the Primary and Junior schools.

The day began with a speech by the headteacher. She welcomed everybody and **(20)** .... the programme for the day.

Then we had the running races in one part of the sports **(21)** .... and the other events in another part. There were winners for each event, but there were also points for the second and third person, which **(22)** .... to their teams. It was a very close competition, but in the end the Red Team got the most points. The captain of the Red Team **(23)** .... a cup from the headteacher, which the team keeps until the next Sports Day.

At the very end of the day, there was a teachers' football match, which was very funny. Some of the teachers dressed up in strange costumes and they didn't **(24)** .... the rules properly, which made everyone laugh.

19	A	watch	B	hear	C	see
20	A	told	B	explained	C	said
21	A	place	B	field	C	land
22	A	went	B	came	C	gave
23	A	had	B	became	C	received
24	A	do	B	make	C	follow

Part 5

Questions 25 – 30

For each question, write the correct answer.
Write **ONE** word for each gap.

Example: | 0 | having |

To	Sophia
From	Sarah

Hi

We're **(0)** .... a party at my house for my sister's birthday and my parents said I **(25)** .... invite one person, so I chose you! I hope you're free that day. It's next Saturday, **(26)** .... is the 8th, I think, at 3.00 at our house. You needn't bring a present **(27)** .... she'll get hundreds from all our cousins! If the weather's nice, we will have it in the **(28)** .... , but we'll go ahead even **(29)** .... it's raining because we've got a big living room, as you know.

Can you let me know as soon as possible if you'll be **(30)** .... to come?

Sarah

Part 6

Question 31

You are going to go to the zoo with your English friend Pat next Saturday. Write an email to Pat.

Say:

- where you want to meet
- how you are going to get to the zoo
- what you want to do at the zoo

Write **25 words** or more.

Part 7

Question 32

Look at the three pictures.
Write the story shown in the pictures.
Write **35 words** or more.

9.00 a.m.

1.00 p.m.

4.00 p.m.

Cambridge A2 Key

Reading and Writing

Test 3

© 2025 Prosperity Education.
'Cambridge A2 Key' and 'KET' are brands belonging to The Chancellor, Masters and Scholars of the University of Cambridge and are not associated with Prosperity Education or its products.

Part 1

Questions 1 – 6

For each question, choose the correct answer.

1

School Trip
If you have booked for the school trip next Monday, you must come to a meeting in the hall at lunchtime. We have important information to give you.

A   Students who are interested in the school trip are meeting at lunchtime in the hall.

B   Students must go to the hall at lunchtime to hear about the school trip.

C   There is a meeting of students who are going on the school trip at lunchtime in the hall.

2

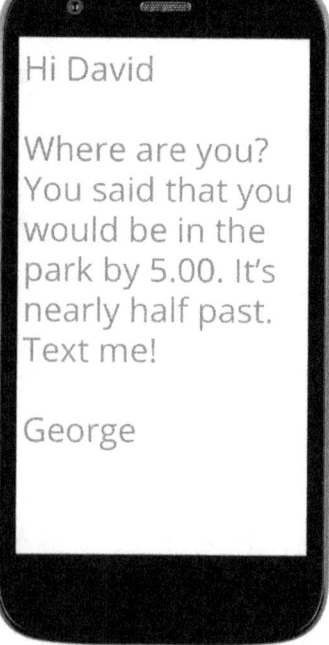

Hi David

Where are you? You said that you would be in the park by 5.00. It's nearly half past. Text me!

George

What should David do?

A   go to the park

B   send George a message

C   meet George in half an hour

3

Contact numbers
You can contact the school during office hours [8.00–5.00, Mon–Fri, including lunchtimes] on 01202 777864. At any other time, call 01202 777546.

You can contact the school office

A   on 01202 777864 at lunchtime on weekdays.

B   on 01202 777546 at lunchtime on weekdays.

C   on 01202 777864 at the weekend.

4

To: Emma
From: Sarah
Hi

You know we have to send a copy of our passport to the school for the Geography trip. Well, which email address should we use? Is it the main office one or the Geography teacher's?

Sarah

Sarah needs to know

A   where to send a copy of her passport.

B   whether she has to send a copy of her passport to the school.

C   how many copies of her passport she has to send.

5

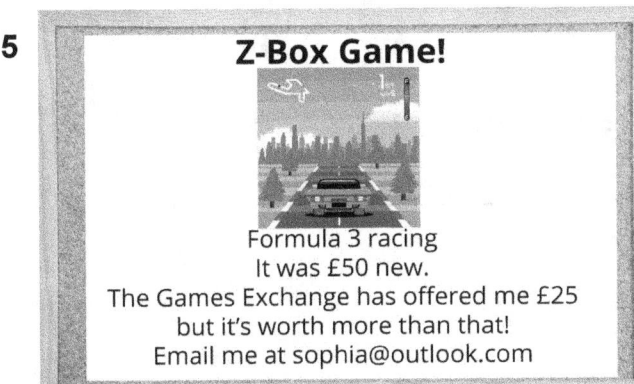

Z-Box Game!
Formula 3 racing
It was £50 new.
The Games Exchange has offered me £25 but it's worth more than that!
Email me at sophia@outlook.com

The person who is selling this game

A   wants £25.

B   wants more than £25.

C   wants £50.

6

Dear Parent,

Please note that from Monday 23rd February, the school café will no longer accept cash. Your child will only be able to buy food after that date with a plastic card.
Your child must:
1 get a café card from the school office;
2 give the receptionist some money to put on the card.

From February 23rd, children can

A   only buy food from the café with cash.

B   get a plastic card from the café.

C   only use a café card to buy food.

Turn over ▶

Part 2

Questions 7 – 13

For each question, choose the correct answer.

		Helen	Vicky	Zoe
7	Who comes from a large family?	A	B	C
8	Who has a younger sister?	A	B	C
9	Whose chores are on a list?	A	B	C
10	Whose chores include looking after the pets?	A	B	C
11	Who shares with her sister?	A	B	C
12	Who has to do things twice sometimes?	A	B	C
13	Who doesn't know where everything goes in the kitchen?	A	B	C

What chores do you have?

We asked three students how they help around the house.

Helen

I think I do a lot, but my mother says I don't. I make my bed every day and I try to keep my room tidy, but it's difficult because my sister is in the same room and she's very messy. She's only six, though. I always help with the washing-up after a meal, but I'm no good at putting things away in the right place. At the weekend, I help with the washing. I quite like putting things on the line when the weather's good.

Vicky

I don't like doing chores, but I know they're important. I've got three brothers and two older sisters, so my parents get a lot of help. Of course, we make a lot of mess, too. We each have a set of jobs which are on a piece of paper in the kitchen. I am responsible for collecting the rubbish from each room and taking it out to the bins. I also have to clean one of the bathrooms once a week, which I hate.

Zoe

There isn't a lot to do in our small flat. It's just me and my mother. But she wants everything to be perfect, so she often tells me to clean something again when I think it's fine. We've got two dogs and a cat, and my special job is making sure they have food at the right times and that they always have water. I have to clean up if they make a mess, too, like bringing mud in from the garden on a rainy day.

Turn over ▶

Part 3

Questions 14 – 18

For each question, choose the correct answer.

She's 21 – and she has been to every country in the world

There are 195 countries in the world in the United Nations list and Alexis Alford, or Lexi to her friends, has visited all of them. Very few people have done that anyway, but Lexi is only 21.

By the time Lexi was 12, she knew that she wanted to be an explorer. Perhaps she became interested because her parents worked in the travel business. They taught her to find out about places before going. They also showed her how to book plane tickets and hotels. They took her to a lot of countries when she was a teenager. She went to 72, actually, by the age of 18.

Lexi did a number of jobs while she was still at school. She saved money for her later travels without her parents. But she also learnt in those years that, if you find out about foreign places before you go, you can travel the world at a low cost.

While she was visiting more than 120 countries between 18 and 21, she made some money by writing a diary and selling her photographs through her website. However, she did not need a lot of money because she travels light with only the important things in a backpack. She buys the cheapest plane tickets and doesn't stay in expensive hotels.

Of course, she had a number of problems during her travels. Sometimes police officers would not let her into a country at first, but in the end she always got the stamp in her passport. She also had some health problems on the way, including getting sick from eating bad food. She missed her home after only three months away.

She finally completed her amazing journey in North Korea on May 31st, 2019. At the time of writing, she is the youngest person to visit every country, which earns her a place in the *Guinness Book of World Records*.

14   How did Lexi learn about travel planning?

   A   from travel agents

   B   from her parents

   C   from travelling before the age of 18

15   What did she learn from her years of travelling with her parents?

   A   You can do international travel cheaply.

   B   You need to find out a lot of information about a country before you go there.

   C   You should research a new place well when you get there.

16   How did she pay for her travels?

   A   with savings and with money from her website

   B   with money that she earned through the internet

   C   with savings from jobs when she was living at home

17   Why did she sometimes have trouble getting into a country?

   A   She couldn't get permission at first.

   B   She didn't have the correct kind of passport.

   C   She had the wrong stamp in her passport.

18   Why is Lexi in the *Guinness Book of World Records*?

   A   because she has visited every country in the UN list

   B   because she visited North Korea in May 2019

   C   because she is the youngest person to visit all the countries in the world

Turn over ▶

Part 4

Questions 19 – 24

For each question, choose the correct answer.

After-school clubs

Would you like to **(19)** .... some fun straight after school? Join one of our after-school clubs and you can! We have something for everyone.

If you like sports, there's a football club. **(20)** .... the first half hour, you learn a new skill **(21)** .... passing the ball. Then, in the second half hour, there are five-a-side games.

If you **(22)** .... board games, we have a chess club. You learn famous moves from international chess competitions, and then you play two or three games to practise your new skills.

Finally, for nature lovers, we have a birdwatchers club. If the weather is bad, we study films of birds in their natural environment. You learn how to **(23)** .... birds from their shape and their colours. On fine afternoons, we go out into the park behind the school, watch real birds and listen to their **(24)** ....

Come to the hall today at 4.00 and choose your club!

19	A	get	B	have	C	do
20	A	During	B	While	C	With
21	A	like	B	such	C	example
22	A	wish	B	want	C	prefer
23	A	watch	B	recognise	C	prefer
24	A	songs	B	music	C	sounds

Part 5

Questions 25 – 30

For each question, write the correct answer.
Write **ONE** word for each gap.

Example: | 0 | getting |

| To | Katy |
| From | Holly |

Hi Katy

I'm looking forward to **(0)** .... back to school next week! I have **(25)** .... so bored at home for the last three weeks. At first, it was quite fun **(26)** .... I didn't have any pain, but my temperature was high. The doctor saw me and said I should **(27)** .... go to school in case I gave something to other people.

Anyway, I'm better now, **(28)** .... I'll see you on Monday. I'm sure there will **(29)** .... a lot of school work for me to catch up on! I hope you'll tell me **(30)** .... things are really important.

Holly

Part 6

Question 31

It is World Book Day tomorrow. You must go to school as a character from a book. Write an email to your English friend, Sam, about it.

Say:

- which character you are going as
- why you are going as that character
- what you are going to wear

Write **25 words** or more.

....

....

....

....

....

Part 7

Question 32

Look at the three pictures.
Write the story shown in the pictures.
Write **35 words** or more.

....

....

....

....

....

....

Cambridge A2 Key

Reading and Writing

Test 4

Part 1

Questions 1 – 6

For each question, choose the correct answer.

1

Green Monday!
Up to 50% discount
for one day only!
Come into our store
on Monday 1st May
and get many things at half price.
[Note that discounts are not available from our online store.]

On Monday 1st May,

A   you can buy some things in store at 50% discount.

B   you can buy everything at this store at half price.

C   you can order many things from the online store at 50% discount.

2

Hi Helen

I know you wanted to see that new film but I've just checked the cinema website. It's not on until next week! So do you still want to meet this evening? Let me know.

Sarah

What should Helen do?

A   tell Sarah when the new film is on

B   suggest somewhere to go this evening

C   say whether she wants to meet Sarah this evening

3

Food in classrooms
You must not eat food at lunchtime in the classrooms. We have to keep the rooms clean for the afternoon lessons.
Please go to the school café to eat your sandwiches.

This notice is for

A   all students.

B   students who have lunch in the school café.

C   students who bring their own lunch.

4

To: Betty
From: Sophia

Hi

Have you done the Maths homework yet? I can't work out the answer to number 7. I'm sure it's 15 but I can't explain it.

Sophia

Sophia wants to know

A   why the answer to number 7 is 15.

B   whether the answer to number 7 is 15.

C   what the correct answer to number 7 is.

5

Textbook for sale!

Are you in Year 3?
Are you studying history?
Do you want the textbook
at a low price?
Contact me on 07799 621345.

Call the number

A   if you are in Year 3.

B   if you are studying history.

C   if you want to buy the history textbook.

6

Writing competition

Get your entry forms from the school office today!
Two prizes:
8–12: stories of 150 to 200 words
13–16: stories of 200 to 300 words
Hand in your stories before 22nd September.

David is 10. He wants to enter the competition. must write

A   at least 150 words.

B   more than 200 words.

C   exactly 200 words.

Turn over ▶

Part 2

Questions 7 – 13

For each question, choose the correct answer.

		Richard	Harry	Michael
7	Who does his homework on the way home?	A	B	C
8	Who doesn't meet school friends at the weekends?	A	B	C
9	Who feeds animals after school?	A	B	C
10	Who likes reading about planets and astronauts?	A	B	C
11	Who sometimes goes fishing in his spare time?	A	B	C
12	Who uses the web during his free time?	A	B	C
13	Whose parents live above their shop?	A	B	C

What do you do in your free time?

We asked three students how they spend their free time.

Richard

I don't have a lot of free time in the week because I work in my parents' shop after school. I spend most of the time putting things on shelves.

Then, I go upstairs to our flat and do my homework. I always have the radio on while I'm working. The music helps me concentrate.

When I have finished my homework, I play with my school friends in the park or I read if I have got a good book about space from the school library. I'm not on social media.

Harry

When I get home from school, I help my parents on their farm. There's always lots to do with the animals. I like feeding them, so I think it's part of my free time!

After the farm work, I usually just do my homework and go to bed. If I don't have any homework, I watch television in my bedroom. I have a laptop for school, but we can't get the internet on our farm.

At the weekend, there are more jobs to do around the farm, but my parents won't let me work at all on Sunday, so I get up late, then I go and meet my school friends. Then we fish in the river on our farm, but we never catch anything!

Michael

My home is a long way from the school. I travel by train and it takes about 45 minutes, so I have lots of time to do my homework. When I get home, I'm free to play in the garden with my brother or go on my laptop. There's always something funny to read or watch on one of the social media sites.

I sometimes get bored at the weekends because none of my school friends live near me. But my father always takes me and my brother out on Sunday afternoon. Sometimes we go to the river and Dad fishes while Peter and I go swimming.

Turn over ▶

Part 3

Questions 14 – 18

For each question, choose the correct answer.

The 100-year-old lamp ... and its inventor

In a fire station in California, there is a light bulb. It is only special in one way. It was turned on for the first time in 1901, so it has been in use for nearly 120 years. That's more than one million hours. At first, the fire officers turned the light on and off in the normal way, but they never turn it off now because they are afraid that it will not turn on again. They do not even clean it anymore.

The bulb has become famous around the world, and it has its own website where you can actually see the bulb in use. It is at http://www.centennialbulb.org/photos.htm#anchor1234. It is called an Edison bulb because the design is from an invention by Thomas Edison.

Edison was born in the USA in 1847. He did not go to school. His mother taught him at home. From an early age, he worked. Most children did at that time. He sold sweets and newspapers on the trains near his home. At the same time, he did experiments and began to invent things. While he was still a child, he became deaf in one ear and then lost some of his hearing in the other ear after an illness. But he said it was easier to work when he didn't have lots of sounds around him.

Edison did not only invent the light bulbs which we use today. He invented more than 1,000 new devices, including a machine which recorded sound and a machine which recorded movement – the film camera.

Edison was famous for spending as much time as he needed to solve a problem. When an experiment failed for the hundredth time, he said, 'I haven't failed. I have found 100 ways which don't work.'

14 Why don't the fire officers turn the bulb off?

    A   They don't want to clean it.

    B   They don't know if it will turn on again.

    C   They know it won't turn on again.

15 Why is it called an Edison bulb?

    A   because Edison made it

    B   because Edison turned it on in 1901

    C   because it is based on an Edison invention

16 Why did Edison work from an early age?

    A   It was normal when he was young.

    B   He wanted to make money for his parents.

    C   He needed money for his experiments.

17 How did Edison feel about his deafness?

    A   It helped him in his work.

    B   He thought it was a good thing.

    C   He liked being deaf.

18 What did Edison mean when he said 'I haven't failed'?

    A   My experiment was a success.

    B   Nobody could make this experiment work.

    C   I have learnt some things which don't work.

Turn over ▶

Part 4

Questions 19 – 24

For each question, choose the correct answer.

Study Camp!

Do you want to spend time with your school friends this summer? Would you like to get better **(19)** .... in your tests in the autumn? Are you interested in team sports like football and basketball? Do you get bored **(20)** .... the long summer holidays?

If you **(21)** .... 'Yes' to any of these questions, Study Camp could be the answer for you!

You can stay with us for two, three or four weeks and have fun while you learn. Study Camp **(22)** .... just £200 per week, including all your food. In the morning, you have lessons with teachers who **(23)** .... every class interesting. In the afternoon, we have sports competitions. Every evening, we build a fire and have a barbecue if the weather is fine. If it is raining or cold, we serve **(24)** .... food in the camp restaurant.

Go to the school office today and tell the receptionist that you want to go to Study Camp this summer!

19	A	points	B	marks	C	numbers
20	A	during	B	while	C	through
21	A	replied	B	said	C	answered
22	A	prices	B	earns	C	costs
23	A	make	B	do	C	get
24	A	beautiful	B	delicious	C	sweet

Part 5

Questions 25 – 30

For each question, write the correct answer.
Write **ONE** word for each gap.

Example: | 0 | taken |

To	William
From	Robert

Hi William

Well, we are here but it has (0) .... more than 12 hours. First, the plane took off more than two hours late (25) .... there was snow on the runway. Then the pilot told (26) .... that the runway at Borgen Airport was closed (27) .... we had to go to Hammelfest, (28) .... is more than 50 kilometres north. But (29) .... we arrived, the hotel receptionist said that the snow on the ski slopes is perfect, so the skiing (30) .... be good tomorrow.

More tomorrow!

Robert

Part 6

Question 31

It's your birthday next Monday. You want to go out with your English friend Jo for a special meal. Write an email to Jo.

Say:

- where you want to go

- what you want to eat

- what you want to do after the meal

Write **25 words** or more.

Part 7

Question 32

Look at the three pictures.
Write the story shown in the pictures.
Write **35 words** or more.

Cambridge A2 Key

Reading and Writing

Test 5

© 2025 Prosperity Education.
'Cambridge A2 Key' and 'KET' are brands belonging to The Chancellor, Masters and Scholars of the University of Cambridge and are not associated with Prosperity Education or its products.

Part 1

Questions 1 – 6

For each question, choose the correct answer.

1

> **End of term**
> The summer term will end at 2.30 on Thursday 14th July. Bring a letter from your parents if you want to go home at that time, or wait for the buses at 4.00 in the normal way.

On 14th July,

A   all the students can go home at 2.30.

B   students must wait until 4.00 for their bus.

C   students who want to go home at 2.30 must bring a letter from their parents.

2

Hi Betty

What's the name of the Maths website which you told me about? Email me the link so I can just click it.

Thanks

Holly

What should Betty do?

A   text Holly the name of the website

B   call Holly and tell her the name of the website

C   send Holly an email with the name as a link

3

> **New email address**
> Please note that after 11th February, the address of the school will be westschool@outlook.com. The address westschool@gmail.com will stop working on 25th February.

It's 10th February. How can you contact the school by email?

A   on westschool@outlook.com

B   on westschool@gmail.com

C   on either of the addresses

4

> New Message
> To Harry
> From George
> Hi
>
> What shall we do after school? I wanted to see Space Team but it isn't on at the ABC Cinema until next week.
>
> George

George wants

A   a suggestion from Harry for this afternoon.

B   information about the film *Space Team*.

C   information about the ABC Cinema.

5

Skateboard for sale!

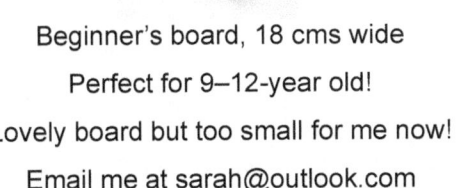

Beginner's board, 18 cms wide
Perfect for 9–12-year old!
Lovely board but too small for me now!
Email me at sarah@outlook.com

Who is this skateboard good for?

A   Clare is 10. She is a very good skateboarder.

B   Lily is 12. She has never been on a skateboard.

C   Julia is just starting to skateboard. She is 10.

6

Dear Parent,

We have sent a number of children home this week because they have a high temperature and stomach problems.

Please do not send your child to school if you think they might be ill. Just email the school office to let us know that your child will be away.

Mrs Smith
Headteacher

The headteacher wants

A   to know if a child is ill.

B   to send home children who are ill.

C   to stop children who are ill coming to school.

Turn over ▶

Part 2

Questions 7 – 13

For each question, choose the correct answer.

		Robert	Frank	William
7	Who gets up at the normal time on Saturday	A	B	C
8	Who has a cooked breakfast?	A	B	C
9	Who eats lunch with his parents?	A	B	C
10	Who goes to the school on Saturday?	A	B	C
11	Who doesn't work on Saturday?	A	B	C
12	Who never plays football on Saturday?	A	B	C
13	Who sometimes goes to a restaurant for dinner?	A	B	C

My Saturdays

We asked three students to talk about a normal Saturday.

Robert

I usually get up at about 9.00 on Saturday. My mother cooks something for me, like boiled eggs or bacon. I try to do my school work for Monday on Saturday morning, but if one of my friends is doing something interesting, I may go and see him.

On Saturday afternoon, I make some sandwiches for lunch then I leave home. I'm in our football team, so I need to get to the school playing field by 2.00 and it's quite a long way from my house.

I get home at about 4 or 5 and have a snack. Then we sometimes go round to my grandparents' house – they live quite close – and we have dinner there.

Frank

I have a paper round to get pocket money, and the newspapers come out on Saturday as well as every weekday, so I can't stay in bed later. Luckily, I don't deliver the Sunday papers!

So I get up at 7.00, have a piece of toast and a glass of milk and I get on my bike at about 7.30.

After my job, I'm quite tired – there are a lot of hills on my paper round, so I lie on the sofa and watch television if there's a baseball game on, but I read instead if they show a football game.

In the evening, we usually have a family meal, either at home or we go to a fast food place.

William

My parents have a shop which is open on Saturday, and I work there in the mornings to earn some money. The shop opens at 7.00, but my parents let me stay in bed a bit longer at the weekend, so I go down to help at about 9.00 after having some cereal and orange juice. I work in the shop all morning, then we shut the shop for an hour and go upstairs to have lunch.

If it's fine, I go to the park with my friends in the afternoon. We play football or just talk. If it's raining or cold, I go to one of my friends' houses to play computer games. The shop shuts at 7.00 and we have a family meal in the kitchen.

Part 3

Questions 14 – 18

For each question, choose the correct answer.

The eagle which flew to the Moon

On 20th July, 1969, something amazing happened. A man climbed down from a door to the ground. It was amazing because the door was on a small spaceship, the man was an astronaut and the ground was the Moon.

The man's name was Neil Armstrong. Another astronaut, Buzz Aldrin, waited in the small spaceship while the third person in the team, Michael Collins, was in a large spaceship above the Moon.

Four days before, at 9.32 a.m. on July 16th, the three men took off from the Earth. It took 76 hours to travel the 390,000 kilometres from the Earth to the Moon. The large spaceship went round the Moon while a small spaceship called *Eagle* went down to the Moon. More than 500 million people watched the event on television as it happened. They heard Armstrong say 'The *Eagle* has landed.'

Armstrong and Aldrin stayed on the Moon for two and a half hours. They collected rocks and took photographs. They then returned to the large spaceship and began the journey back to the Earth. They arrived back on 24th July and landed in the ocean near the island of Hawaii.

There were another six journeys to the Moon in the next three years. For the last three visits, the astronauts took a car which could travel over the rocky ground of the Moon. This meant that they could explore large areas of the Moon around the landing site.

In total, 12 men have walked on the Moon, including Armstrong and Aldrin, but no human has walked on the Moon since 1972. Only American astronauts have ever walked on the Moon, but several countries, including China, India and Japan, have sent spacecraft to the Moon without humans on board.'

14 Why was the man's action amazing?

    A   because the man was climbing down from a spacecraft

    B   because the man was an astronaut

    C   because the man was stepping onto the Moon

15 Where was the main spaceship on the 20th July, 1969?

    A   It was on the Moon.

    B   It was about halfway to the Moon.

    C   It was very close to the Moon.

16 What did Collins do while the *Eagle* was on the Moon?

    A   He went round the Moon in the main spaceship on his own.

    B   He waited in the *Eagle* with Aldrin.

    C   He went round the Moon in the main spaceship with Aldrin.

17 How far did the main spaceship travel in July 1969?

    A   390,000 kilometres

    B   780,000 kilometres

    C   more than 780,000 kilometres

18 Which of these sentences is true, according to the text?

    A   No spaceships have been to the Moon for 50 years.

    B   No one has ever driven a vehicle on the Moon.

    C   No Chinese astronauts have ever gone on the Moon.

Turn over ▶

Part 4

Questions 19 – 24

For each question, choose the correct answer.

School Science Fair

Every year we have a science fair for the students in Year 6. It takes **(19)** .... over three days, and it is always a huge success. Students from all the other years come **(20)** .... the three days.

You can work on your **(21)** .... or in a small group. First, you must think of a question to answer, for example, 'How can you stop an ice cube from melting?' Then you must think of some **(22)** .... answers, like, 'Put it in a metal bucket, or a plastic glass, or put it in a towel.' Then **(23)** .... an experiment to find the answer.

Last year, the winner was the balloon car. Emma Jones asked the question: 'How far can a model car **(24)** .... with the power of a balloon?' Her balloon car was beautifully made and painted, and it went much further than she expected!

19	A	part	B	place	C	room
20	A	during	B	while	C	with
21	A	own	B	self	C	team
22	A	could	B	can	C	possible
23	A	have	B	do	C	make
24	A	travel	B	trip	C	journey

Part 5

Questions 25 – 30

For each question, write the correct answer.
Write **ONE** word for each gap.

Example: | 0 | ago |

To	Anna
From	Helen

Hi

So here we are in our new house! We actually moved two days **(0)** .... , but I couldn't get the internet working in my bedroom **(25)** .... now. I really **(26)** .... it here, but I woke up the first morning and I didn't know **(27)** .... I was! I thought I was in a hotel room **(28)** .... the room looked so different.

After two days, it still feels very strange, **(29)** .... I'm getting to know where everything is.

You must come and stay here during the summer holidays. We've **(30)** .... plenty of room for guests now.

Love

Helen

Turn over ▶

Part 6

Question 31

You are going to go and meet your English friend Charlie in the town centre at the weekend. Write an email to Charlie.

Say:

- what time you want to meet
- where you want to go
- what you want to do

Write **25 words** or more.

Part 7

Question 32

Look at the three pictures.
Write the story shown in the pictures.
Write **35 words** or more.

....

....

....

....

....

....

Cambridge A2 Key

Reading and Writing

Test 6

© 2025 Prosperity Education.
'Cambridge A2 Key' and 'KET' are brands belonging to The Chancellor, Masters and Scholars of the University of Cambridge and are not associated with Prosperity Education or its products.

Part 1

Questions 1 – 6

For each question, choose the correct answer.

1

School meal tickets

The tickets for school meals are now available from the school office. You need a ticket to get lunch in the restaurant. The lunch people cannot take cash.

A   If students want school meals, they can get tickets in the restaurant.

B   Students must get their school meal tickets before going to the restaurant.

C   Students can buy meals in the restaurant.

2

Hi Betty

When did we agree to meet today at Jack's house? Was it before or after lunch? Text me.

Holly

What should Betty do?

A   text Holly the time of the meeting

B   text Holly the meeting place

C   meet Holly for lunch at Jack's house

3

School shop

Open Mon–Fri
10.15–10.30
11.15–11.30
2.15–2.30
Friday: Everything half price!

At the shop, you can buy things at

A   half price at 2.00 on Friday.

B   normal price at 10.25 on Monday.

C   normal price at 2.20 on Friday.

4

To: Harry
From: George

Hi

I can't get into the school homework club! I've got the user name but I've forgotten the password.

George

George wants

A the user name and password for the homework club site.

B the user name for the homework club site.

C the password for the homework club site.

5

Bike for sale!

Lovely pink bike with basket on front. I rode to school every day for two years but it's too small for me now!
Email sophia@outlook.com

Why is Sophia selling the bike?

A She needs a bigger bike.

B She has bought another bike.

C She doesn't ride to school anymore.

6

School play

Would you like a part in this year's school play? Come to a meeting in the hall at 1.00 on Wednesday. We need actors and people to help with lights, music and so on.

The meeting is for

A people who want to act in the play.

B people who want to help with the play.

C actors and helpers.

Turn over ▶

Part 2

Questions 7 – 13

For each question, choose the correct answer.

		Emma	Sally	Vicky
7	Whose friend suggested that she should enter the competition?	A	B	C
8	Who won a prize with a photo of her pets?	A	B	C
9	Whose friends always choose the photograph which she enters?	A	B	C
10	Who won a prize with a funny photograph?	A	B	C
11	Who won a prize with a photograph of an insect?	A	B	C
12	Whose mother and father chose the photograph to enter?	A	B	C
13	Who couldn't get a good picture of autumn trees?	A	B	C

The school photograph competition

We talk to this year's winners.

Emma

I've never entered a competition like this before and I nearly didn't enter this time. My friend told me to enter and I thought, 'Why not?'

I didn't have any good photos on my phone, so I went out into our garden early one morning and I took hundreds of photos – flowers, trees, birds. I even photographed a bee and a snail!

I showed the photos to my parents and they said the best one was the bee. My mother loved the way it was sitting on a flower. I didn't think I had a chance but I entered and I won first prize.

Sally

I won the prize last year with a photo of my grandmother, but I didn't want to photograph a person this time. It took me a long time to decide on a subject. I tried taking some pictures of the river near our house, but I couldn't get a good photograph. So then I thought about the trees on the way to school. They were beginning to turn red and brown and yellow. They looked beautiful, but the school bus was going so fast that the pictures were awful.

Finally, I saw it. There was an old car in a drive and a bird was looking out of the window. It made everyone laugh, and I got second prize for it.

Vicky

I always enter this competition but I've never won anything before, so I'm really pleased. I take photographs all the time of people and things in nature, like leaves and flowers. I choose four or five of my favourites and then I show them to my friends. I let them decide on the best one. This time, most of them chose a photo of my dog and my cat. They don't really like each other, but I managed to get a photo of them lying together in front of the fire.

I'm proud of my third prize, but I want to get first prize next year.

Turn over ▶

Part 3

Questions 14 – 18

For each question, choose the correct answer.

The most interesting person I've ever met

Robert talks about his grandfather, Oliver.

I love talking to my grandfather about his life. It seems like he has been to every country in the world. I think he has done every job, so he has hundreds of wonderful stories.

My grandfather had to leave school at 14 to get a job because his father was out of work. The family lived near the sea and my grandfather got his first job carrying things off the ships.

After a few months, one of the people who sailed the ships said, 'I need a young man to help on my next journey to Brazil.' My grandfather went with him. His first journey by sea was very long. The ship stopped in Spain and then several places in Africa. He had many adventures in the cities there. He did all sorts of jobs on the way to Brazil, including cooking and catching fish. He also learnt how to make the engines work.

The ship finally arrived in Brazil after three months. When Oliver got to Brazil, he decided that he wanted to stay there for a while, so he got a job on a coffee farm. He clearly learned fast. The man who owned the farm was called Ronaldo and he lived a long way away, so after a while, he made Oliver the manager. He had to learn how to run a company very quickly, and he became very good at buying and selling things.

One day, Ronaldo told my grandfather that he was too old to travel anymore and he needed someone to look after all his companies, not just the coffee farms all over Brazil. So, at the age of 25, my grandfather became one of the most important businessmen in South America, Africa and Asia.

So that was the beginning of my grandfather's life. And I want to start my life in the same way.

14 Why is Robert's grandfather the most interesting person Robert has met?

    A   because he has been to every country in the world

    B   because he tells interesting stories

    C   because he has had lots of jobs

15 Where did Oliver have many adventures?

    A   in Spain

    B   in Brazil

    C   in places in Africa

16 Where did Oliver learn to cook?

    A   on the ship

    B   in Africa

    C   in Brazil

17 Why did Oliver have to learn to run a company quickly?

    A   because the owner lived a long way from the plantation

    B   because he became a manager very quickly

    C   because he was a fast learner

18 What did the owner of the coffee farm ask Oliver to do when Oliver was 25?

    A   look after all the farms in Brazil

    B   look after the companies in South America

    C   look after his companies in three continents

Turn over ▶

Part 4

Questions 19 – 24

For each question, choose the correct answer.

School Teams

Would you like to play in one of our school teams and help us win competitions this year?

We have teams for football, basketball and baseball. We have **(19)** .... teams for each sport, so there is something for everyone. If you have never played a sport, we teach you the basic rules of the game and how to play it well. After some **(20)** .... , we might choose you to play for the school. If you have a lot of experience, you can go into a team **(21)** ....

Our teams play all the other schools in the city on Saturday mornings. Sometimes we play at our school and sometimes we play on other playing **(22)** .... If we are playing at home, come to the school at 10.00. If we are playing somewhere else, you don't need **(23)** .... There will be buses to take you to the game.

If you are interested, come to the school hall on Wednesday and join one of the sports teams. It's fun and you learn to work with **(24)** .... people.

19	A	several	B	few	C	number
20	A	day	B	time	C	age
21	A	learn	B	immediately	C	increase
22	A	courts	B	grounds	C	fields
23	A	transport	B	trip	C	travel
24	A	another	B	other	C	some

Part 5

Questions 25 – 30

For each question, write the correct answer.
Write **ONE** word for each gap.

Example: | 0 | written |

To	Julia
From	Helen

Hi

How are you? Sorry I haven't **(0)** .... for a few days, but I couldn't get on the internet at first in our new house. But it's working now, so here I am!

The new school is fine but I miss my friends, especially you! As you know, I **(25)** .... worried about riding my bike to school, but actually, I don't **(26)** .... it at all. It's **(27)** .... closer than before and it's easier **(28)** .... I don't have to get the school bus.

The thing **(29)** .... I like best about the new school is the teachers. They are lovely! That's all for now. I **(30)** .... write again at the weekend.

Love

Helen

Turn over ▶

Part 6

Question 31

You have agreed to go shopping with Sam on Saturday.
Write an email to Sam.

Say:

- when you want to meet

- where you want to meet

- what you want to buy

Write **25 words** or more.

Part 7

Question 32

Look at the three pictures.
Write the story shown in the pictures.
Write **35 words** or more.

Cambridge A2 Key

Reading and Writing

Test 7

Part 1

Questions 1 – 6

For each question, choose the correct answer.

1

Found!

Scarf left in school restaurant last Thursday lunchtime.
You can get it back from the school office if you can describe it! A photo of you wearing it is even better.

If someone wants to get the scarf back,

A   he/she can take it from the school office.

B   he/she must give details of the colour(s) and length to the office staff.

C   he/she must show a photograph of it.

2

Hi Matt

I can't make it for our football practice at 4.00 this afternoon in the park. Is 4.30 too late?

Phone or text me.

George

What should Matt do?

A   tell George the time of the meeting

B   tell George if he will still be there at 4.30

C   tell George where to meet him at 4.30

3

C2
Change of room: Please go to Room A1 at 2.00 today.

Thank you!
Mr Smith

C3
Your class will be in this room at 3.00 as normal.

Students in C3

A   should go to Room A1.

B   should come to this room instead of Room A1 at 3.00.

C   do not need to do anything different today.

4

To: Katy
From: Sarah

Hi

What's the book that the teacher talked about this afternoon? She said it's in the school library. It's called something like 'The Science of Food'. I know it's by Jane somebody.

Sarah

Sarah wants to know

A   the full name of the book.

B   the user name for the homework club site.

C   how to get a copy of the book.

5

West Street Chemist's
Sorry!
We are closed!
Opening hours: 9–5, Mon–Sat
If you need to contact us out of hours call 01020777816.

Eva needs medicine. It is Sunday. What should she do?

A   go to the chemist's between 9 and 5

B   wait until Monday

C   call the telephone number

6

Do not ride your bicycle here!

Robert wants to use this road. What can he do?

A   ride his bicycle

B   get off his bicycle and push it

C   carry his bicycle

Turn over ▶

Part 2

Questions 7 – 13

For each question, choose the correct answer.

		Betty	Holly	Helen
7	Who put notes in her diary in the past?	A	B	C
8	Who writes times of important things in her diary?	A	B	C
9	Who will use her phone for times of important things in the future?	A	B	C
10	Who writes information about homework in a special book?	A	B	C
11	Who can check things to do on a list?	A	B	C
12	Whose parents make sure she remembers things?	A	B	C
13	Who has emails from herself on her phone?	A	B	C

How do you remember things?

We asked three students to talk about their method.

Betty

I always get a diary from my parents for my birthday and I write things in there. For example, my diary for this week says for Monday: '3.00 Dentist' – I'm not looking forward to that. Then for Wednesday, I have '6.30 Football' – I'm going to see our local team with my father.

But sometimes I forget to look at my diary, so I'm going to start using the calendar on my phone. Then it will play a tune or something when it is time to go to the dentist or the football match.

Holly

When I was younger, I wrote everything in my diary, but I never took it with me in my bag so I kept forgetting things. So now I put everything on my phone. I've got an app for notes and, of course, there's the calendar app. But if it's something long, like homework, I send an email to myself.

Of course, I can't use my phone at school, so I have to remember to put things like homework and meetings with friends in my phone on the way home. So sometimes I write notes on pieces of paper and put them in my bag. And sometimes, I find the notes days later and I think, 'Oh, dear! I didn't go to that meeting on Monday lunchtime!'

Helen

I don't really need to remember anything around the house because my mother always tells me, 'Don't forget to make your bed,' or my father says, 'Remember to feed the cat.' There is also a list of jobs for me to do on the fridge, so every time I go to get a drink, I think, 'Oh, no! I haven't tidied my room yet.'

At my school, we have homework books and the teachers make sure we fill them in at the end of every lesson, so I can't forget my homework.

Turn over ▶

Part 3

Questions 14 – 18

For each question, choose the correct answer.

How do you spend your free time?

Most people have quite a lot of free time now. For example, in America, most adults have about five hours of free time each day. A report this year says that they spend nearly three hours watching television. They spend about one hour meeting friends and playing computer games. So they only have one hour left for every other activity, like playing sports or reading. In fact, they only spend about 20 minutes a day on sports, so adults in America spend too much time sitting down and not doing exercise.

There are some differences in free-time use for different groups of people. First, the level of education seems to be important. For example, people who have been to university watch less television than people who left education after school. Why do we find this difference? Perhaps television programmes are more interesting for people with a lower level of education. And perhaps university-level people spend their free time playing sports and doing exercise.

Second, the age of a person seems to be important. Television is the main free-time activity for both young people and old people. But old people in the USA watch nearly twice as much TV as teenagers. American teenagers spend much more time than older people playing computer games. They also contact their friends more through the internet. Older Americans spend more time than teenagers reading and doing nothing. Why do we find these differences? Perhaps many older people do not have computers.

Some people are worried about all the time which people spend sitting down. We need to take exercise every day to keep our bodies healthy. People sit down during most of the day at school, at university and in most modern jobs. It is important for us to spend some time walking and running in our free time if we want to stay healthy.

14 How much of their free time do most American adults spend watching television?

    A   a third

    B   a half

    C   more than a half

15 What does the writer think about 20 minutes' exercise a day?

    A   It's not enough.

    B   It's enough.

    C   It's too much.

16 What does the writer say about people with a high level of education?

    A   They have been to university.

    B   They don't watch as much television as other people.

    C   There are no interesting television programmes for them.

17 What reason does the writer suggest for older people watching more television than younger people?

    A   Many of them don't like playing computer games.

    B   They prefer watching television.

    C   Many of them might not have a computer.

18 How is watching television the same as studying, playing computer games and reading?

    A   They are all free-time activities.

    B   You do all the activities sitting down.

    C   Both teenagers and older people do all these activities.

Turn over ▶

Part 4

Questions 19 – 24

For each question, choose the correct answer.

Local Area Studies

Dear Student

Perhaps the teacher has told you that your class will soon begin to work on a project about a **(19)** .... place. It could be a shop with a long **(20)** .... You can talk to the people who are in the shop now, and the people who have **(21)** .... the shop in the past. If you choose to study a park, you could photograph the flowers, the birds and the insects which live there, and find out **(22)** .... it is a good place for them. You will work in teams of six and you must make sure that each person has a **(23)** .... to do.

At the end of the project, you must make a poster which your teacher will **(24)** .... in the classroom. You will talk about your place to the rest of the class.

The teacher will put you into teams on Monday, but start thinking about interesting places now!

19	A	local	B	near	C	nearby
20	A	age	B	history	C	time
21	A	lived	B	owned	C	bought
22	A	why	B	reason	C	how
23	A	work	B	job	C	thing
24	A	put on	B	put away	C	put up

Part 5

Questions 25 – 30

For each question, write the correct answer.
Write **ONE** word for each gap.

Example: | 0 | but |

| To | Mary |
| From | Sophia |

Hi

We're here! It was a long journey **(0)** .... it was fun. The plane took off about half an hour late and we **(25)** .... through a storm. I was a little frightened at first, but the pilot came on the radio and made **(26)** .... jokes. My parents picked up our car at the airport and we drove to the hotel, **(27)** .... is quite close to the beach. It took us about two hours to get there. The journey was boring, but the hotel looks just **(28)** .... in the photos, so that's good. I think we **(29)** .... have a great time here. I'll write tomorrow **(30)** .... we get back from the beach.

Love,

Sophia

Turn over ▶

Part 6

Question 31

You have agreed to meet with an English friend, Tom, for a drink in a café. Write an email to Tom.

Say:

- where you want to go
- why you want to go there
- when you want to go

Write **25 words** or more.

Part 7

Question 32

Look at the three pictures.
Write the story shown in the pictures.
Write **35 words** or more.

Cambridge A2 Key

Reading and Writing

Test 8

Part 1

Questions 1 – 6

For each question, choose the correct answer.

1

Closed
We are open:
Mon–Fri: 7.00 a.m.–11 p.m.
Sat: 7.00 a.m.–7.00 p.m.
Lunch break: 1.00 p.m.–2.00 p.m.
call 01020777816.

You cannot buy things from this shop

A   before 10.00 on Saturday.

B   after 5 p.m. on a weekday.

C   any day at 1.30 p.m.

2

New Message
To   May
Cc
From   Ellen   Bcc
Hi

Do you remember who we should give the Science project to on Monday? I can't remember if it's the Physics teacher or the Chemistry teacher.

Ellen

Send

Ellen wants

A   the name of a teacher.

B   information about the Science project.

C   to know where to take her Science project.

3

Homework Club

The Homework Club this week will not be in the hall because we are working on the school play. Please go to the library instead.

A   Students who are not in the play must go to the hall.

B   Students who go to the Homework Club should go to the library this week.

C   The Homework Club will be in the hall after the play.

4

Bicycle helmet!

Only £8 (New = £20)
Come to my classroom any lunchtime and try the helmet on.
Peter C4

A   You can buy this helmet for £20.

B   Peter wants more than £8 for the helmet.

C   This helmet cost Peter £20.

5

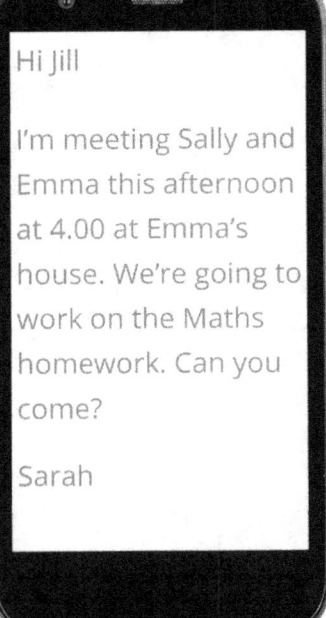

Hi Jill

I'm meeting Sally and Emma this afternoon at 4.00 at Emma's house. We're going to work on the Maths homework. Can you come?

Sarah

What should Jill do?

A   go to Emma's house at 4.00

B   tell Sarah if she can come to Emma's house at 4.00

C   ask Sally if she can come to Emma's house at 4.00

6

The School Band

We need more people for the band!
If you can play the guitar, the piano or the drums, come to the hall at lunchtime on Wednesday.
[We're choosing singers in the hall on Thursday.]

A   Anyone can join the school band.

B   If you are a singer, you should go to the hall on Wednesday lunchtime.

C   If you play a musical instrument, go to the hall on Wednesday lunchtime.

Turn over ▶

Part 2

Questions 7 – 13

For each question, choose the correct answer.

		Anna	Clare	Jo
7	Who didn't follow her mother's suggestion?	A	B	C
8	Who has only written one poem in her life?	A	B	C
9	Who learnt about the competition from her mother?	A	B	C
10	Whose friends chose the poem to send in?	A	B	C
11	Who wrote about changing the way we look at things?	A	B	C
12	Whose poem is funny?	A	B	C
13	Whose poem started as a song?	A	B	C

Poetry competition

Send us your poem [up to 50 lines] with some information about you and where the idea came from.

Anna

I'm Anna and I'm 14. I'm in a band with three of my friends and I write most of the songs. One of the other girls saw the information about the competition and said that my songs were really poems so I should send in one of those. I couldn't decide which one to send, so the girls picked one for me. It is about a young girl who has to go and live in another country when her mother gets a new job.

Clare

My name is Clare and I'm 12. I write poetry all the time but I've never entered a competition before. I show everything to my mother, and she wanted me to send in one about my pet dog. But I think that one's a bit silly, so in the end I chose my latest one. I got the idea from a short story which I read. Someone comes from another planet. She has learnt English but she makes a lot of mistakes which make people laugh.

Jo

My name is Jo. I'm 11. My mother saw the information about this competition when she came to pick me up from school one day. She knew that I loved reading poetry, so she said I should start writing it! I found it quite easy and I wrote my poem immediately. It's about a girl who thinks that everything in her life is bad – her home, her parents, her school. Then she sees a programme on television about a child who has a really hard life, and suddenly her own life looks different. I haven't written another poem yet.

Turn over ▶

Part 3

Questions 14 – 18

For each question, choose the correct answer.

The best teacher I've ever had
by Jane Collins, age 14

I have had a lot of good teachers in my life. They have been good in different ways. The kindest teacher was actually my first teacher. I was very unhappy for the first few weeks, but she helped me make friends. I can't remember her name because we just called her Miss.

The funniest person was Mr Jones. He was my class teacher in my last two years at my first school when I was 10 and 11. He didn't tell funny stories or say things in a funny way, but we laughed all the time. I don't know why! I was sad when I had to leave the first school and get a lot of new teachers.

But some of them at my next school were very good. One of the best teachers at my second school taught History. Sometimes History can be very boring, with a lot of names and dates, but Miss Brooks didn't teach like that. She made everything into a story. And she asked us for ideas. For example, she might say, 'So the people were very angry with the king because the price of food was very high. So what did they do?' We suggested things, then she told us what really happened. I loved that way of teaching.

I had a good Maths teacher once, Mr Brown, who turned everything into a project. So when we were learning about measurements, like metres and centimetres, he made us get up and go out into the school car park to measure it. Then we had to measure a car and say how many cars could park in the car park. Again, we were learning, but we were having fun at the same time.

So I have had some very good teachers in my life. But when I thought very hard about the question: 'Who is the best teacher you've ever had?', I knew that there is only one person. She is called Mrs Collins and she is kind and funny, asks for my ideas all the time and teaches me while we're having fun. She's my mother, of course.

14 Why did Jane like her first teacher?

- A because she was kind
- B because she was like her mother
- C because she wasn't married

15 How did Mr Jones make learning fun?

- A He told jokes.
- B He used funny voices.
- C She doesn't know.

16 Why wasn't History boring with Miss Brooks?

- A She taught names and dates well.
- B She asked the children to suggest things.
- C She had lots of interesting ideas.

17 Why did Mr Brown make them measure the car park?

- A to see how many cars could park there
- B to learn about centimetres and metres
- C to make them stand up and go outside

18 Who is the best teacher that Jane has ever had?

- A Miss Brooks
- B Mr Brown
- C her mother

Turn over ▶

Part 4

Questions 19 – 24

For each question, choose the correct answer.

Lake Summer Camp

Do you get bored in the long summer holidays? Is there no one to play with in your area? Would you like to **(19)** .... fun with children of your own age?

If you have answered 'Yes' to any of those questions, then Lake Summer Camp is for you! Children of all ages from 8 to 17 **(20)** .... to us for up to four weeks in July and August.

Our camp is in a forest near a beautiful lake. Every morning, we go out to the lake to swim or windsurf. In the afternoon, we play team games **(21)** .... football and basketball. In the evening, we often have a **(22)** .... with burgers and sausages. At night, you sleep in warm tents with children of your own age. It's a bit **(23)** .... sometimes because you can hear the animals in the forest, but none of them are **(24)** .... !

Tell your parents today: 'I want to go to Lake Summer Camp this summer!'

19	A	make	B	do	C	have
20	A	arrive	B	come	C	get
21	A	like	B	example	C	as
22	A	picnic	B	meal	C	barbecue
23	A	scary	B	frightened	C	worried
24	A	bad	B	dangerous	C	horrible

Part 5

Questions 25 – 30

For each question, write the correct answer.
Write **ONE** word for each gap.

Example: | 0 | are |

To	Fred
From	Robert

Hi

How (0) .... you? I'm on a cruise ship (25) .... *Queen of the Sea*, and I'm writing to you next to the pool, (26) .... is wonderful. The ship is enormous and it (27) .... everything – restaurants, cinemas, a theatre, a library and, of course, a swimming pool. We are (28) .... to stop at a small town tomorrow and we can get off the boat and explore, which (29) .... be great. I'll take some photos and send them (30) .... you with my next email.

Robert

Turn over ▶

Part 6

Question 31

You are going to go shopping with your English friend Pat on Sunday. Write an email to Pat.

Say:

- where you want to meet
- what time you want to meet
- what you want to buy

Write **25 words** or more.

Part 7

Question 32

Look at the three pictures.
Write the story shown in the pictures.
Write **35 words** or more.

Cambridge A2 Key

Reading and Writing

Test 9

Part 1

Questions 1 – 6

For each question, choose the correct answer.

1

School Play

If you have offered to help with the school play next week, you must come to a meeting in the hall at lunchtime today.
We have important information to give you.

A Students who are interested in the school play are meeting at lunchtime in the hall.

B Students must go to the hall at lunchtime to hear about the school play.

C There is a meeting of students who want to help with the school play at lunchtime in the hall.

2

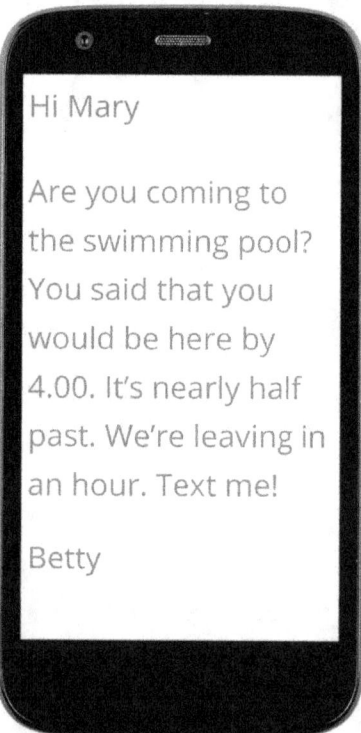

Hi Mary

Are you coming to the swimming pool? You said that you would be here by 4.00. It's nearly half past. We're leaving in an hour. Text me!

Betty

What should Mary do?

A go to the swimming pool

B say sorry to Betty

C tell Betty if she is coming to the pool

3

To Sophia
From Helen

Hi

Have you done your work on the Science project yet? We have to give it in on Friday. If you need any help, call me.

Helen

Helen needs to know

A if Sophia wants any help with the Science project.

B if Sophia knows that they have to give in the Science project on Friday.

C if Sophia knows when they have to give in the Science project.

4

Mountain Dogs Concert
I have two tickets for this great group on February 13th ... but I can't go! They cost me £15 each but I'll take £10.
Email me at jim546@outlook.com

The person who is selling these tickets

A   wants £10.

B   wants £15.

C   wants £20.

5

Dear Parent,

Please note that from Monday 18th January, your child will only be able to enter the school with a plastic card.
Your child must get his or her card from the school office during the week beginning January 11th.

Children must get their cards from the school office

A   on 11th January.

B   between 11th January and 15th January.

C   when they enter the school.

6

School shop
Open during all breaks
Mon–Thu:
10.15–10.30
12.30–1.30
3.15–3.30
Fri: Closed from 1.30

You can buy things at this shop

A   at 1.00 on a Wednesday.

B   at 3.15 on a Friday.

C   at 12.00 on a Tuesday.

Turn over ▶

Part 2

Questions 7 – 13

For each question, choose the correct answer.

		David	Robert	Paul
7	Who buys his hobby things from a shop?	A	B	C
8	Who does his hobby outdoors?	A	B	C
9	Who gets things for his hobby from the web?	A	B	C
10	Who keeps his hobby things behind glass?	A	B	C
11	Who keeps his hobby things in books?	A	B	C
12	Who likes bird song?	A	B	C
13	Whose hobby things might be worth a lot of money?	A	B	C

What is your favourite hobby?

We asked three students to tell us about their hobby.

David

I live in the country, so every morning I wake up to the sound of birds. I love it and perhaps that's why I love watching birds. My interest started when I was young. I found a baby bird while I was cycling and I took it home and looked after it. Finally, it got better and one day it flew away. I wasn't sad. I was happy that I could help. Now I have lots of books which help me to give names to the birds which I see. Every weekend I go out to the forest behind our house and I watch the birds and take photos of them with my phone.

Robert

I got my hobby from my grandfather. When I was about 10, I stayed with my grandparents and he showed me his stamp collection. I didn't really understand at first, because nobody sends letters anymore. That means it's not really possible to collect stamps from letters which you receive. So I go online and look for interesting stamps for sale. I was a birdwatcher when I was younger, and now I collect stamps with birds on them. I have got a few expensive stamps in my albums, which are books with plastic wallets to keep the stamps clean. I didn't pay a lot of money for them, because many people don't know how unusual some stamps are.

Paul

I have a strange hobby. At least, all my friends say it is strange. I like collecting model cars. I don't mean models of modern cars. They all look the same, but old cars are different. There are lots of different shapes. I really like American cars from the 1950s. Some of them look like spaceships. When I am old enough, I want to buy an old American car. I don't play with the cars. I don't want to take the paint off them or make any marks on them. I have them in my bedroom in a cupboard with glass doors. I bring them home from the model shop and put them straight in the cupboard and just look at them.

Turn over ▶

Part 3

Questions 14 – 18

For each question, choose the correct answer.

The best country I've ever visited
by Grace White

I'm not very old but I've already been to quite a lot of countries. My mother is a pilot, so she flies all over the world and she gets cheap tickets, or even free tickets, for everyone in the family.

My parents took me to my first foreign country when I was only two. They say that we went to France for a few days. I don't remember anything about it.

The first place I remember is Spain, which we went to on holiday when I was five. The hotel had a beautiful pool. For the first few days, I spent all the time jumping in and out. Finally, I got earache. Perhaps the water was dirty. We had to get some medicine from a chemist's. I had to watch all the other kids playing in the pool after that.

When I was six, we flew – cheaply! – to the Caribbean area and went on a big ship for two weeks. We spent a lot of time on the ship, but we also stopped at several different countries. So I have been to Guadeloupe, Dominica, Jamaica and Mexico. I couldn't tell you which was which except for the last one because I remember the exciting music. I also loved the delicious food.

During the next six years, I went to countries in North Africa and South America, and it was there that I fell in love with a country – Brazil. I love the music and the food there! But most of all, I love the wonderful things from nature which you can see – the beaches, the jungles, the mountains and the huge waterfalls. And of course, all the animals. We stayed in one hotel and every night as we were eating our dinner, very small monkeys came down slowly from the trees until they were sitting on our table and taking pieces of our food. I took some cool photos on my phone. It is the best country I've ever visited and I can't wait to go back.

14 How many countries does Grace name?

　A　seven

　B　eight

　C　nine

15 Why doesn't she remember anything about France?

　A　She only went there for a short time.

　B　She was too young.

　C　She has been to so many countries.

16 Why did she have to stop using the pool in Spain?

　A　She got ill.

　B　The water was dirty.

　C　There were too many children in the pool.

17 Which country does she remember from the Caribbean area?

　A　Guadeloupe

　B　Jamaica

　C　Mexico

18 Why is Brazil the best country she has ever visited?

　A　because the food is delicious

　B　because the music is exciting

　C　because the natural things are wonderful

Turn over ▶

Part 4

Questions 19 – 24

For each question, choose the correct answer.

Drama Club

Do you like acting? Would you like to **(19)** .... your acting skills and have fun? Every Wednesday, we meet in the school hall straight after school for one hour. We have two groups. The first one is for children between 8 and 11 and the **(20)** .... for children between 12 and 15.

Sometimes we read parts of a play, **(21)** .... famous ones like *Romeo and Juliet*. Sometimes we are scary animals or robots! Sometimes we play scenes which we **(22)** .... For example, last week everybody had to be doctors and nurses in a hospital and we had lots of funny conversations.

Once a year, the older children do a play for people to come and **(23)** .... Last year, we did parts of a funny play called *Educating Rita* about a woman who did not have a good **(24)** .... but goes to a summer school and finds out that she is really very clever.

19	A	increase	B	improve	C	better
20	A	second	B	two	C	twice
21	A	including	B	like	C	example
22	A	make	B	think	C	invent
23	A	watch	B	go	C	look
24	A	education	B	learn	C	school

Part 5

Questions 25 – 30

For each question, write the correct answer.
Write **ONE** word for each gap.

Example: | 0 | enjoying |

| To | Claire |
| From | Alice |

Hello from London!

I'm really **(0)** .... our weekend in the capital city! Yesterday, we went to London Zoo. Have you ever **(25)** .... there? If not, you should go, **(26)** .... there is so much to see. You can't see everything in a few hours, of course, but we **(27)** .... lions and leopards and giraffes. We saw some small animals **(28)** .... , like the little hippos. But my favourites were the pandas, **(29)** .... were beautiful!

We're **(30)** .... to go to a museum tomorrow. I hope it's as good as the zoo!

Alice

Turn over ▶

Part 6

Question 31

It is Clean Town Day next Sunday. You must do something to make your town cleaner. Write an email to your English friend, Jo, about it.

Say:

- what you are going to clean

- how you are going to clean it

- what you would like your friend to do

Write **25 words** or more.

Part 7

Question 32

Look at the three pictures.
Write the story shown in the pictures.
Write **35 words** or more.

Cambridge A2 Key

Reading and Writing

Test 10

© 2025 Prosperity Education.
'Cambridge A2 Key' and 'KET' are brands belonging to The Chancellor, Masters and Scholars of the University of Cambridge and are not associated with Prosperity Education or its products.

Part 1

Questions 1 – 6

For each question, choose the correct answer.

1

Next term

The autumn term will begin on Tuesday 12th September. Please do not come to school on Monday 11th. This is a staff training day.

Teaching staff

A   will be teaching on 11th September.

B   will be at the school on 11th September.

C   will not be at the school on 12th September.

2

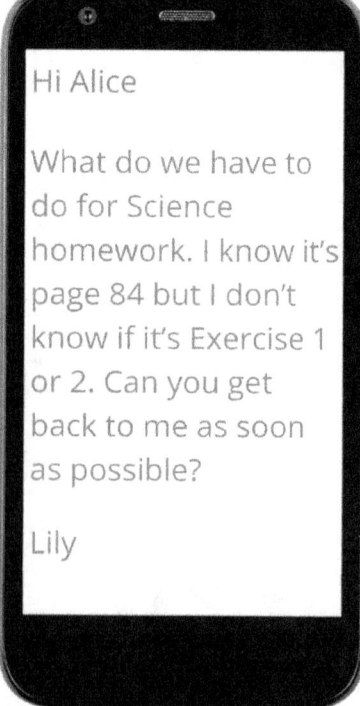

Hi Alice

What do we have to do for Science homework. I know it's page 84 but I don't know if it's Exercise 1 or 2. Can you get back to me as soon as possible?

Lily

What should Alice do?

A   call Lily and tell her the correct page number

B   text Lily with the answers to the Science homework

C   email, call or text Lily with the correct exercise number

3

We use these gates
24 hours a day
7 days a week!

We will take away bicycles which are in front of the gates.

This notice means that

A   you can leave your bicycle here.

B   you can't leave your bicycle here because people sometimes take bicycles.

C   you can't leave your bicycle here because people need to open the gates.

4

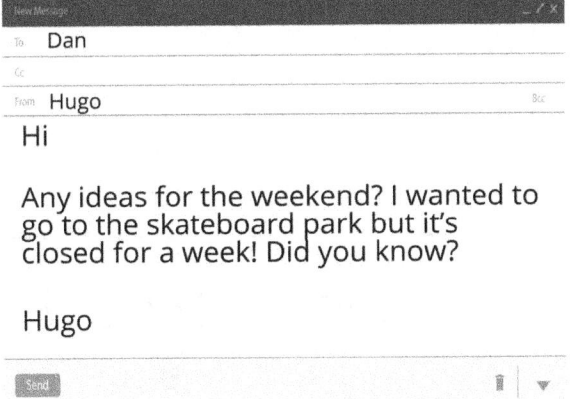

To Dan
From Hugo

Hi

Any ideas for the weekend? I wanted to go to the skateboard park but it's closed for a week! Did you know?

Hugo

Hugo wants

A information about the skateboard park.

B a suggestion from Dan for the weekend.

C to go to the skateboard park.

5

Mountain bike

Nearly new.
It cost £135 two years ago.
Make me an offer!
Email me at sophia@gmail.com

Sophia wants

A to know the price which people will pay.

B people to pay at least £135 for the bike.

C £135 for the bike.

6

Dear Parent,

We have heard that there will be heavy snow on Friday this week. If it snows on Thursday night, please phone the school to check if we are open or not.

Mr Green
Headteacher

Parents should

A not take their children to school on Friday.

B call the school on Friday morning before bringing children in case there is snow.

C take their children to school on Friday if there is no snow on Thursday night.

Turn over ▶

Part 2

Questions 7 – 13

For each question, choose the correct answer.

		Jack	Paul	Tom
7	Who didn't do a painting?	A	B	C
8	Who used a lot of different colours?	A	B	C
9	Who usually paints animals?	A	B	C
10	Who chose the subject of the painting quickly?	A	B	C
11	Who didn't follow his mother's suggestion?	A	B	C
12	Who chose a person as the subject?	A	B	C
13	Who painted several pictures then chose one?	A	B	C

Art competition

The winners of this years' competition talk about their paintings and drawings.

Jack

It took me a long time to decide what to do. I usually do horses and dogs and cats, but I wanted to do something different for the competition. My mother said, 'You could paint those apples and oranges in the bowl,' but I thought that was boring. In the end, I chose a woman who lives in my village. She's very old and she's got an interesting face. You can see all the experiences she has had. I used a pencil instead of paints. It seemed better in this case.

Paul

As soon as I heard about the competition, I knew what I wanted to paint, but my mother was surprised when she saw it, because I've never done an animal before. But he's my dog and he's lovely and I've always wanted to paint him. I waited until he was sleeping so he didn't move around a lot. I only used brown and white, because he's brown and white and his bed is brown. Oh, and a little bit of black.

Tom

We live by the sea, so a lot of my paintings show the people on the beach and the men in their fishing boats. People think that the sea is blue, but it isn't only blue. Sometimes it's grey or green and sometimes it looks red and orange when the sun is going down. I painted the same picture again and again, but the one I sent in was from a sunny summer evening. It had all the colours from my paintbox in it.

Turn over ▶

Part 3

Questions 14 – 18

For each question, choose the correct answer.

The Internet of Things (IOT)

We know that the internet joins computers together around the world. Through the internet, I can talk to you by email. We know that the World Wide Web joins information sites and online shops to the internet. Through the web, I can find information and buy things. But there is so much more to come! It's called the Internet of Things, or IOT.

Many people in IT believe that 20 billion things will be part of the internet in the next few years. You may already have some things inside your home joined to your home network. For example, many people have internet music speakers. But in future, washing machines, heating and air-conditioning units could also join. Your fridge might become part of a network with your rubbish bin. They might talk to a shopping website. You might not have to think about shopping again. Every time you use something, like milk, your fridge will check how much is left. Every time you throw something away, your rubbish bin will read the bar code. Then it will add that item to your online shopping list. Perhaps it will even order the item and pay for it.

Outside your home, your family car may already have maps joined to the internet. If you are late for a meeting, your family car, your bicycle or even your shoes might be able to check your phone calendar and send a message to the person you are meeting: 'Sorry. I will arrive in 28 minutes.' Of course, your car, bicycle or shoes will know where you are going and the traffic which you will meet on the way.

IOT has an exciting future, but it is also a scary one. Some people say that the answer is not to join things to your home network, or not to join your network to the internet. But if you do that, you miss all the good things about IOT. It is better to use future IT but also to have very good passwords to make it safe.

14 What do we use to buy things online?

- A the internet and the World Wide Web
- B the World Wide Web
- C the internet

15 How quickly will the Internet of Things grow, according to the texts?

- A very quickly
- B quite quickly
- C quite slowly

16 How could a rubbish bin help with shopping?

- A It could check everything which you throw away.
- B It could add items to your shopping list as you throw them away.
- C It could tell you how much is left of everything.

17 How could your shoes say how late you will be if they were on the Internet of Things?

- A They could check how fast you are walking and how far it is.
- B They could check the traffic with a maps app.
- C They could look at your phone calendar.

18 How can we stop bad things happening through the Internet of Things, according to the text?

- A Don't join things to your home network.
- B Don't join your home network to the internet.
- C Don't use poor passwords on your home network.

Turn over ▶

Part 4

Questions 19 – 24

For each question, choose the correct answer.

The Robot Race!

Every year we have a robot race for the students in Year 6. It takes **(19)** .... for one hour after school every day for a week, and it is always a lot of fun. Students from all the other years **(20)** .... and choose their favourite robot to win.

If you are in Year 6, your science teacher will **(21)** .... to you next week how robots work. You can build a robot on your **(22)** .... or in a small group. But all the robots must be able to walk, and the fastest robot of all will win!

You can use up to three batteries. Robert Smith won the **(23)** .... last year with a funny orange robot which moved very fast. It fell over a few times, but in the end it was the **(24)** ....

19	A	part	B	place	C	room
20	A	come	B	arrive	C	become
21	A	explain	B	tell	C	say
22	A	self	B	own	C	team
23	A	test	B	quiz	C	competition
24	A	winner	B	first	C	top

Part 5

Questions 25 – 30

For each question, write the correct answer.
Write **ONE** word for each gap.

Example: | 0 | ago |

To	Lucy
From	Daisy

Hi

I'm sending you with this email the first pictures of my new pets. They are lovely! They're only eight weeks old. I actually got them three days **(0)** .... but I've been too busy looking after them **(25)** .... send you an email. They didn't sleep **(26)** .... the first two days, so I'm really tired. But I think they're happier now. I was **(27)** .... to buy one, but I'm glad I decided to get two. It was a bit scary at first **(28)** .... I kept losing them. They're so small that they **(29)** .... get into a shoe or under the sofa. I often don't know **(30)** .... they are. They're making a noise now, so I think they want food. More later!

Love

Daisy

Part 6

Question 31

You are going to go to meet your English friend Charlie in the park next Sunday. Write an email to Charlie.

Say:

- what time you want to meet

- what you want to do

- where you want to have something to eat

Write **25 words** or more.

Part 7

Question 32

Look at the three pictures.
Write the story shown in the pictures.
Write **35 words** or more.

Answers

Practice Test 1 Reading and Writing

Part 1   6 marks

1   C
2   A
3   C
4   A
5   B
6   C

Part 2   7 marks

7   A
8   C
9   B
10   A
11   B
12   A
13   C

Part 3   5 marks

14   B
15   A
16   C
17   A
18   B

Part 4   6 marks

19   B
20   A
21   C
22   B
23   A
24   C

Part 5   6 marks

25   in
26   is
27   to
28   where
29   some / them
30   which

Part 6   15 marks

Hi Jo,

Can we meet at the bus stop on Saturday and then go to the sports centre? I can get there at 10.00. I'd like to play tennis.

See you soon.

Part 7   15 marks

I went camping with my friends at the weekend. We went to a beautiful place near a river. I fished in the river and caught a fish. Then we made a fi e and we cooked the fish

Practice Test 2 Reading and Writing

Part 1	6 marks
1	A
2	A
3	B
4	A
5	B
6	B

Part 2	7 marks
7	A
8	B
9	B
10	C
11	A
12	C
13	C

Part 3	5 marks
14	B
15	C
16	B
17	B
18	C

Part 4	6 marks
19	A
20	B
21	B
22	A
23	C
24	C

Part 5	6 marks
25	could
26	which
27	because
28	garden / yard
29	if
30	able

Part 6   15 marks

Hi Pat,

Can you come to my house by about 9.00 on Saturday because my mother wants to leave at 9.30? I want to see the big cats. What about you?

Part 7   15 marks

Mr and Mrs Smith moved house at the weekend. The lorry came early in the morning. The men put everything in the lorry. They took everything to the new house and carried it in. By 4 in the afternoon, they could sit down and watch television.

Practice Test 3 Reading and Writing

Part 1		6 marks
1	C	
2	B	
3	A	
4	A	
5	B	
6	C	

Part 2		7 marks
7	B	
8	A	
9	B	
10	C	
11	A	
12	C	
13	A	

Part 3		5 marks
14	B	
15	A	
16	C	
17	A	
18	C	

Part 4		6 marks
19	B	
20	A	
21	A	
22	C	
23	B	
24	A	

Part 5		6 marks
25	been	
26	because	
27	not	
28	so / and	
29	be	
30	which	

Part 6   15 marks

Hi Sam,

I'm going to go as Robinson Crusoe. He is my favourite character in my favourite book. I'm going to wear a piece of cloth over my T-shirt and I've got a plastic parrot.

Part 7   15 marks

Last week, Mr and Mrs Brown went out with their children, Tom and Sue. They walked beside the river with their dog. They were very tired when they got home in the evening. They had dinner in the kitchen.

Practice Test 4 Reading and Writing

Part 1		6 marks
1	A	
2	C	
3	A	
4	A	
5	C	
6	A	

Part 2		7 marks
7	C	
8	C	
9	B	
10	A	
11	B	
12	C	
13	A	

Part 3		5 marks
14	B	
15	C	
16	A	
17	A	
18	C	

Part 4		6 marks
19	B	
20	A	
21	C	
22	C	
23	A	
24	B	

Part 5		6 marks
25	because	
26	us	
27	so	
28	which	
29	when	
30	should	

Part 6   **15 marks**

Hi Jo,

I'd like to go to the burger place in the shopping centre next Monday. I want to have a cheeseburger with chips. Shall we go to the cinema after the meal?

Part 7   **15 marks**

Bill, Eva and Michael had a race in the park. Bill and Eva ran very fast and they were close to each other for a long time. But Bill won the race in the end. Eva was second. She was just in front of Michael.

Practice Test 5 Reading and Writing

Part 1		6 marks
1	C	
2	C	
3	B	
4	A	
5	C	
6	C	

Part 2		7 marks
7	B	
8	A	
9	C	
10	A	
11	A	
12	B	
13	B	

Part 3		5 marks
14	C	
15	C	
16	A	
17	B	
18	C	

Part 4		6 marks
19	B	
20	A	
21	A	
22	C	
23	B	
24	A	

Part 5		6 marks
25	until	
26	like	
27	where	
28	because	
29	but	
30	got	

Part 6   15 marks

Hi Charlie,

Are you still OK to meet at the weekend? I can get to the town centre by 10.00. Shall we meet on the corner of North Street? I'd like to go to the shopping centre.

Part 7   15 marks

My friends and I went to the beach on Sunday morning. The beach was very dirty. There was plastic everywhere. We decided to tidy the beach. We picked up all the rubbish and put it into bags. At the end of the day, the beach was tidy.

Practice Test 6 Reading and Writing

Part 1   6 marks

1 B
2 A
3 B
4 C
5 A
6 C

Part 2   7 marks

7   A
8   C
9   C
10 B
11 A
12 A
13 B

Part 3   5 marks

14 B
15 C
16 A
17 B
18 C

Part 4   6 marks

19 A
20 B
21 B
22 C
23 A
24 B

Part 5   6 marks

25 was
26 mind
27 much
28 because
29 that / which
30 will

Part 6   15 marks

Hi Sam,

What time would you like to meet on Saturday? I can catch a bus which gets there at 10.00. We can meet at the coffee shop on the first flo . I want to get a new jacket.

Part 7   15 marks

I went on holiday with my family during the summer. We put everything in the car. Then we drove to the beach. We were very happy in the car. It was late when we got to the beach, but we went and ran into the water.

Practice Test 7 Reading and Writing

Part 1 — 6 marks

1. B
2. B
3. C
4. A
5. C
6. B

Part 2 — 7 marks

7. B
8. A
9. A
10. C
11. C
12. C
13. B

Part 3 — 5 marks

14. C
15. A
16. B
17. C
18. B

Part 4 — 6 marks

19. A
20. B
21. B
22. A
23. B
24. C

Part 5 — 6 marks

25. fle
26. some
27. which
28. like
29. will
30. when / after

Part 6 — 15 marks

Hey Tom,

Are you still OK to meet for a drink? I'd like to go to the juice shop in the centre of town. They do fantastic smoothies! I'm free tomorrow afternoon if you are.

Part 7 — 15 marks

My parents went camping with their friends at the weekend. They said that it took a long time to put up the tent. When it was ready, they made a fi e and had something to eat. They were all very tired and went to sleep early.

Practice Test 8 Reading and Writing

Part 1	6 marks
1	C
2	A
3	B
4	C
5	B
6	C

Part 2	7 marks
7	B
8	C
9	C
10	A
11	C
12	B
13	A

Part 3	5 marks
14	A
15	C
16	B
17	B
18	C

Part 4	6 marks
19	C
20	B
21	A
22	C
23	A
24	B

Part 5	6 marks
25	called
26	which
27	has
28	going
29	will
30	to

Part 6 15 marks

Hi Pat,

I'm looking forward to meeting on Sunday. Shall we catch the bus at 9.00 from the stop in front of the library? I want to get a new pair of shoes.

Part 7 15 marks

Tom was nearly ready to leave for school when he saw the bus coming. He went to the bus stop, but then he realized his phone was still in the kitchen. He went back and picked up his phone, but he missed the bus.

Practice Test 9 Reading and Writing

Part 1 — 6 marks

1. C
2. C
3. A
4. C
5. B
6. A

Part 2 — 7 marks

7. C
8. A
9. B
10. C
11. B
12. A
13. B

Part 3 — 5 marks

14. A
15. B
16. A
17. C
18. C

Part 4 — 6 marks

19. B
20. A
21. A
22. C
23. A
24. A

Part 5 — 6 marks

25. been
26. because
27. saw
28. too
29. which
30. going

Part 6 — 15 marks

Hello Jo,

Shall we clean the park on Sunday? There is a lot of plastic on the grass and under the trees. I'll bring some black bags. Can you bring some gloves?

Part 7 — 15 marks

Jill was asleep when her mother came to her bedroom. She told Jill to get up, but Jill went on sleeping. Suddenly, she woke up and realized that she was late. She got everything ready very quickly and ran out of the house. She just caught the school bus.

Practice Test 10 Reading and Writing

Part 1		6 marks
1	B	
2	C	
3	C	
4	B	
5	A	
6	C	

Part 2		7 marks
7	A	
8	C	
9	A	
10	B	
11	A	
12	A	
13	C	

Part 3		5 marks
14	C	
15	A	
16	B	
17	B	
18	C	

Part 4		6 marks
19	B	
20	A	
21	A	
22	B	
23	C	
24	A	

Part 5		6 marks
25	to	
26	for	
27	going	
28	because	
29	can	
30	where	

Part 6 15 marks

Hi Charlie,

Can we meet in the park at 10.00 next Sunday? I'd like to go to the basketball court. There are always a lot of children there who want to play. Then we can get a sandwich from the park shop.

Part 7 15 marks

Ben was at the bus stop at the normal time after school but the bus didn't come. He waited a long time, then he phoned his mother and asked her if she could pick him up. She said yes and arrived a few minutes later.